HOVERCRAFT

by Lisa Bullard

PULL AHEAD BOOKS
Mighty Movers

Lerner Publications Company • Minneapolis

CALGARY PUBLIC LIBRARY

APR   2011

For Robbie and Betsy: Thanks for hovering when it counts! —LB

Copyright © 2007 by Lerner Publications Company

All rights reserved. International copyright secured. No part of this book may be reproduced, stored in a retrieval system, or transmitted in any form or by any means—electronic, mechanical, photocopying, recording, or otherwise—without the prior written permission of Lerner Publications Company, except for the inclusion of brief quotations in an acknowledged review.

Lerner Publications Company
A division of Lerner Publishing Group
241 First Avenue North
Minneapolis, MN 55401 U.S.A.

Website address: www.lernerbooks.com

Words in **bold** type are explained in a glossary on page 30.

Library of Congress Cataloging-in-Publication Data

Bullard, Lisa.
    Hovercraft / by Lisa Bullard.
       p. cm. — (Pull ahead books)
    Includes index.
    ISBN-13: 978-0-8225-6421-8 (lib. bdg. : alk. paper)
    ISBN-10: 0-8225-6421-1 (lib. bdg. : alk. paper)
    1. Ground-effect machines—Juvenile literature. I. Title.
TL718.B85 2007
629.3–dc22   2006018978

Manufactured in the United States of America
1 2 3 4 5 6 — JR — 12 11 10 09 08 07

Hey! Is this a flying saucer going by?

No, it is a hovercraft! Hovercraft are
special machines. They ride on
cushions of air.

Hovercraft can travel over both land and water.

This hovercraft is zooming over ocean waves.

This one is landing on a beach.

Hovercraft can travel over ice and snow.

Shallow water can't stop hovercraft.

Desert sands don't slow down
hovercraft either.

Hang on tight! Hovercraft can even
ride the river rapids.

Hovercraft can go places where boats and cars can't go. So people use hovercraft as **rescue** craft. They bring help to people in trouble.

Armies use hovercraft too. They use hovercraft to move troops and tanks. Hovercraft carry things from ship to shore.

Hovercraft are often used as **ferries**.
Ferries move people and cars across
water.

Some people race hovercraft.

Hovercraft can move very fast on their cushions of air.

Fans force air under the hovercraft.
A **skirt** holds in most of the air. Do you
see the black skirt around the bottom
of this hovercraft?

This hovercraft is parked. The skirt is flat. There is no cushion of air under the skirt.

This hovercraft is moving. Do you see how full the skirt looks? The cushion of air is lifting the hovercraft.

Most hovercraft use **propellers** to move forward. They look like airplane propellers.

The propellers spin and move the air.
The spinning propellers push the
hovercraft forward.

Engines give power to the propellers
and the fans.

The **pilot** turns the engines on and off.
The pilot drives the hovercraft.

The pilot sits in the **cockpit**.

He uses many different controls.

The pilot turns the hovercraft by turning the **rudders** behind the propellers. The rudders steer the hovercraft.

Where will the pilot go next?
Hovercraft can travel almost anywhere!

Fun Facts about Hovercraft

- The world record speed for a hovercraft is more than 85 miles per hour.

- The largest hovercraft ferry held more than 400 people and 60 cars.

- Many people build model hovercraft. They use them on rivers, ponds, and lakes.

- Hovercraft are also called air-cushion vehicles (ACVs).

- Hovercraft are better for the environment than many other moving machines. They do not need to have roads built for them as cars do. They do not harm animals in the water the way boats can.

Parts of a Hovercraft

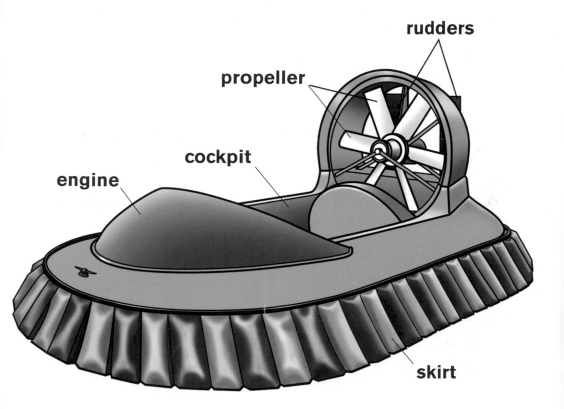

rudders

propeller

cockpit

engine

skirt

Glossary

cockpit: the place where the pilot sits

cushions of air: trapped air that keeps hovercraft above a surface

ferries: hovercraft or boats that carry people and cars across water

pilot: the person who drives the hovercraft

propellers: parts made of spinning blades. Propellers move the hovercraft forward.

rescue: to save from danger

rudders: parts of a hovercraft that are used to turn the hovercraft

skirt: the material around the bottom of the hovercraft. The skirt holds in the air.

More about Hovercraft

Bingham, Caroline. *Big Book of Rescue Vehicles.* New York: Dorling Kindersley Publishing, 2000.

Graham, Ian. *Boats, Ships, Submarines, and Other Floating Machines.* London: Kingfisher Books/Grisewood & Dempsey, 1993.

Hopping, Lorraine Jean. *Flight Test Lab: Hovercrafts.* San Diego: Silver Dolphin Books, 2003.

Solway, Andrew. *Ships.* London: Two-Can Publishing, 1996.

Websites

Dragonfly TV
http://pbskids.org/dragonflytv/show/hovercraft.html
Watch a video segment showing how Rachel and Sara make their own kid-size hovercraft. The girls then ride and test their two models to discover which works best.

Neoterich Hovercraft, Inc.
http://www.neoterichovercraft.com/general.htm
View great photographs of many different kinds of hovercraft. But you may need an adult to help with reading the pages.

Zoom by Kids, for Kids
http://pbskids.org/zoom/activities/sci/hovercraft.html
This website includes directions for making a small hovercraft toy out of simple materials you can find at home.

Index

controls, 25

cushions of air, 4, 16, 18, 19

desert sands, 10

engines, 22, 23

fans, 17, 22

ice and snow, 8

pilot, 23, 24-25

rescue craft, 12

river rapids, 11

shallow water, 9

tanks, 13

Photo Acknowledgments

The photographs in this book are used with the permission of: © Carl & Ann Purcell/CORBIS, front cover; Hovercraft Museum Trust, pp. 3, 4, 5, 6, 8, 10, 11, 17, 18, 19, 20, 21, 22, 24, 26; U.S. Navy Photo, pp. 7, 13, 23, 25, 27; © JENS KOEHLER/AFP/Getty Images, p. 9; AP/Wide World Photos, p. 12; © Tim Hawkins/Eye Ubiquitous/CORBIS, p. 14; © JOHANNES EISELE/AFP/Getty Images, p. 15; © Buzz Pictures/SuperStock, p. 16. Illustration on p. 29 by © Laura Westlund/Independent Picture Service.